I AM THE BUDDHA'S EYES

ALONZO TATE

ISBN: 978-0-578-81995-2

To those who seek and find the truth of their being, may this book be a light to show you the path of the heart through the darkness of suffering.

To the love in which Christ Jesus and the Guru speak.

To the eyes of the Buddha.

I would like to dedicate this book to existence.

To My beautiful queen, it is truly an honor to be in her presence as Jai Ma. You are the heart of the universe itself.

To my mother, my family, and my beautiful kids. I see you all in everything just as I see the one self within all.

I truly want the world to know that truth is everywhere. It doesn't belong to any race, religion or gender. I want all beings to know that you are beyond what you think you are.

CONTENTS

FOREWORD

This collection of wisdom pays great homage to the simplicity of the path to know one's self. My name is Solomon Potter and I am a beloved friend of Alonzo "Good Guru" Tate. This is Alonzo's story of finding the ever-present reality of being. The book began upon meeting Alonzo. As soon as we connected, the space of true friendship and vulnerability laid the soil for Alonzo's story to spring.

Throughout the story, Alonzo describes his journey through conditioning and staying true to himself in the midst of gangs, foster homes, and the adversity of being homeless. The road is never easy but he always managed to feel centered in aloneness. It is almost like falling in love with being alone, for only in aloneness can we truly find and feel our own presence. Self-Inquiry and the most direct spiritual path is the major foundation in which Alonzo realizes the home within himself.

Finding home is the most effortless challenge to feel at peace wherever we may go. This writing will always be dear to my heart and I have found myself in it. Every scene brings us back to the place where we know peace, even when we are faced with the danger of losing everything.

Solomon Potter

CHAPTER 1
MY FIRST AWAKENING

The double-edged sword of discernment was sharpened by the bite of my painful youth.

It's as if I could see the world before it existed and this feeling of detachment kept me alienated from anyone's understanding.

In the spring of 1983, I remember fighting with some kids on the playground. It was the advent of my second year of kindergarten and I was teased for not passing into the 1st grade.

The children were wild and ruthless in San Francisco California. A few boys were ganging up on me because I was different.

I didn't do anything to provoke the cruel acts of the boys, I was simply detached. They came at me throwing punches and attempting to hurt me for not being smart or cool enough - for not being like them.

One of them had bit me on the back like a ravenous dog and I could never forget what happened.

You are that which never changes.
I am that, that never changes.
The pure presence of awareness is the witness
and source of everything.

— GG

The pain didn't faze me, but a shifting in my awareness transpired within. My bodily suffering felt as if it was separate from who I thought I was.

I could see myself outside of my body - the identification with my body - and I just remember this calming presence watching over.

I was completely absorbed in this space of detachment, yet fully present in the scene of being teased. Of course, we got in trouble with the school authorities, but I was more engaged with this new sense of seeing than anything external.

The unveiling of my spirit was the most prominent manifestation in my life at this point. And this seeing has never changed.

Rather than seeing the world through the filter of my 5 year old mind, I had fresh eyes like the lense of a brand new video recorder.

I could see the world as it was without judging it, through an aperture of awareness that allowed the full light spectrum of life to be received in all it's beauty.

You are the silence that is aware. Whenever you think
of yourself, know that you are the pure infinite being;
the unchanging self.

Not as the "I" thought.
Not the personal self, but the supreme awareness.

You are that, I am that.

To awaken you must know that you are that. Abide as that
and one will experience great peace and liberation.

Knowing this will drop all concepts, beliefs and suffering.
It will make no difference what happens to the body
or what thoughts come into your mind.

You are free, timeless, infinite, being. Beyond the body
and beyond the mind - you are pure love itself.

— GG

Happiness and sadness no longer had meaning in my youth, I always felt neutral. All my suffering was still experienced, but it was transmuted into grace. I could never cling to extremes because within my very own witnessing, I was home.

My name was Alonzo Tate. I was a quiet African American boy with long braided hair.

I transferred from school to school because kids would always hurt me, always teased for being aloof. I never had friends that would understand what I was going through.

I always had questions as a child, but never an answer great enough to fulfill me. I felt like a maverick amongst my peers.

There were so many things I wanted to understand about religion, but nothing could satisfy my comprehension.

Where was God? Why can't I see him? Where is heaven? And what is death? I would always ask my grandmother about the big questions of life.

I AM - *is not the presence of a person.*
I AM - *is the presence of the one consciousness that dwells within being as one infinite manifesting aware energy that is the source of all creation.*

— GG

My Grandma was one of my closest friends, but I never got to know her as much as I would like at such a young age.

Bible stories were always entertaining insights in which Grandma shared and elaborated, but I was still searching for truth.

I went to church every Sunday. Each mass had a new lesson to bring to me, though I had so many questions unanswered by the priests.

I wanted to be a good Christian, I wanted to be the best at it. I realized that there was so much to learn in religion but religiousness would never leave me.

My prayers were never answered. I wanted a direct experience of God just like in the bible stories. Jesus had an overflow of love to share and I knew I had the same universal love within me.

No matter how much I begged and asked for God to visit me, he would never come. All I had was this sense that I was being watched over and my new way of seeing could never be altered.

Once one sees what man has made is an illusion
and one's attention has shifted from the mind to presence,

One sees the infinite in all things and
abides within as the witness.

One awakens to one's true nature as
the pure infinite presence of awareness.

— GG

CHAPTER 2
CHILDHOOD CONDITIONING

Life at home was never perfect. My grandmother was mentally ill with schizophrenia and I was never really close to my family, I was only close to my aloneness.

I grew up in the projects. In the ghetto of San Francisco is where I laid my head. It wasn't much, but at least I had a place to be.

My house was a duplex so we lived right next to our neighbors. I remember their dogs were the only friends I had an affinity for.

I would sneak them some food regularly because they were always hungry. They were the only ones I could relate to without feeling judged or like an outsider.

I wasn't thriving in school or at home. I was in and out of different elementary schools, constantly patronized or accused at home, and always alone.

I loved being alone. I felt solace in my own heart. It was never a sad thing for me to be alone but the way in which external life experiences occurred caused me to turn inward.

*The simplest way of awakening back to your natural self
is to just hold onto the sense of* BEING.

Keep the sense of "I" or "I AM" by itself.

*Everyone can do this walking or in meditation position –
it brings immediate results and leads one back to its presence
as the infinite source and witness of all creation.*

— GG

I was always a peaceful boy and it took a lot to shake my quietude.

Being by myself helped me develop my relationship with myself from a very young age. It's not that the world wasn't for me and I was a reclusive sage, but I enjoyed my own company and expanding my understanding of myself.

Growing up as an introverted child allowed me to work on my relationship with God more than anything and that's what differentiated me from other kids.

It's as if I matured faster and could no longer connect with what they were interested in or what they identified with.

I was always so aloof and detached, as if I was in my own world. Not because I was ignoring my reality or didn't want to engage with it, but because I was so curious about my internal world.

It's not like I hated my home, but I was born into a very poor background and everyone was a little insecure within themselves.

The brain and the mind exist.

The mind appears within consciousness as thoughts.

The heart is the light that is awareness.

— GG

My Grandmother's boyfriend was named Warren. Him and I never sat well together. He was into voodoo and witchcraft. His practices brought an eerie aura to my household and that's why I never felt easy about the man.

There were always arguments about spellcasting in my house and I was always the one to be blamed. My auntie Linda and uncle David were living with me too and they would feel bothered by this constant state of paranoia from the practice of witchcraft in the household.

Of course, my Grandmother always found me guilty for certain mishaps around the home. Her schizophrenia was exacerbated with the anxiety of loving a voodoo practitioner. She was always living in a state of fear and so she blamed me for all sorts of phenomena.

If there was something spilled, or there was a giant mess in the living room, or even some mold growing behind the fridge... I was the one to point the finger at.

Awareness does not need a mind to exist.

The "I" which is aware - is prior to mind.

Awareness and mind = pure knowing of the light in which illuminates all experience.

— GG

My innocence was exploited and I was punished for no reason other than false accusation by my own Grandmother. She made me face the leather belt or a simple spanking. I felt so victimized.

At this point in my life, I struggled deeply with my sense of aloneness and at the same time, that is all I wanted... to feel my aloneness.

I felt so out of place, like there was no one in the world experiencing what I was going through and absolutely no one my age who would listen... understand... and relate.

My mother was never present in my life. She was always partying. My mother had me at the young age of 17 and she never really grew up.

She would visit me at my Grandmother's sometimes and I would always look forward to it, but her stays were always short-lived. My mother would come over very briefly to take a bath or get cleaned up... then she was gone again with another guy.

I longed to live with her. I thought that maybe I would have a stronger sense of belonging because I loved my mother very much.

The self is self aware Existence.

There is no other Awareness.

Self is self alone.
There is no one that senses self.
Self is self.
And you are it.

— GG

CHAPTER 3
SHIFTING HOME

I remember running away to find her. Daylight was burning and I was fed up with the way I was being accused at home. I sought out to bring my mother home.

I took bus #5 through the Bay Area to find mom. The bus driver questioned me and asked why a little boy was taking the bus so late by himself, I responded with honesty about my mother and the bus driver empathized with me.

All I could remember was the street that she would always go to with her friend. When my intuition told me the right stop I spoke up and got off.

It wasn't long after walking a few blocks until I finally found the right place!

My mother's friend worked at a shoe shop and I knew I had made it!

I rushed in and found my mother. I greeted her with a big hug and told her how I had been accused of doing spells and witchcraft. I couldn't handle getting whooped anymore.

You are forever pure, you are forever true, and the dream of this world can never touch you - so give up your attachments and give up your confusion.

Realize that peace is beyond all illusions as the pure infinite presence of awareness.

You are timeless bliss.

— GG

Her friend looked puzzled and slightly bothered, my mother was simply concerned. She didn't want me to feel that way but she also was too into her own life to deal with me.

Mother told me I had to return to Grandma's the very next day but I could stay the night in the shoe shop closet.

It was always nice to be tucked in by my mother and fall asleep in her company. She made me feel home again. Her nurturing attitude and energy was what I craved… I knew it wouldn't last.

The next morning I was sent back home.

This was the final stand for my Grandmother because she could no longer take care of me. She was too involved with her own life and I was too into my aloneness.

My family put me into a foster home a month later.

I had never felt so abandoned.

The foster family arrived within a few days of me knowing that I was going into foster care. They were a nice and proper young family with two kids.

A mind full of itself (personhood)
is never present.
A mind that is empty becomes still and shines as awareness.
To awaken is to know that you are knowledge itself and
there's no reason to become anything
because you are perfect
just the way you are.

— GG

I remember the father being a tall calming presence, always wearing dark glasses day and night.

Feeling like a stranger in my own family and being in a new home with people I had no history with made me feel even more of an outsider of my own experience both inward and outward. My aloneness was now magnified by my new unfamiliar surroundings.

Of course, I had no control of my circumstance at this point and I had to conform to the rules of my new family.

There were chores that had to be done and getting used to a new family regime was interesting.

They were called the Corbin family. Their house contained luxurious furniture and the smell had this subtle scent of lavender.

I had my own room and always kept to myself. Again, I was in silent mode and would only speak when spoken to.

When awakening, the mind and
its process will still produce thoughts.

Instead of believing in every thought that appears,
one will become aware when thoughts appear and
one will no longer believe in those thoughts.

This is the shift in realization.

Thoughts only have power
if attention is given.

So when one says remain as yourself,
this means to simply
be the awareness that you are.

— GG

Their children were always favored but I didn't mind. The daughter was really popular and she always wore purple dresses. The son was really cool. He liked to play sports and impress his father - trying to live up to his dad's image and success.

I was adamant about waking up early to go to church. I ended up singing in the choir to honor the name of the Lord. Still, I would rebel through questioning Christianity and stealing all the offerings one time with some buddies.

I was never bothered by the Corbin family, I just didn't relate. It's not like I refused to come down and get to know these people, I was just indifferent and preferred being alone.

They thought I had a disability because I wouldn't speak so they put me into therapy because they felt there was something wrong with me.

My time with the Corbins lasted nearly 5 years. They found out I was smoking weed with their son and felt obliged to kick me out.

In ignorance, you take yourself as a human.

In wisdom, you take yourself as an enlightened being
overflowing with divine music.

As awareness you are neither.

As awareness you are
silence that is eternally aware.

— GG

I always followed their son and he initiated me into smoking at a very young age. Of course the Corbins never believed me because they were convinced the children they raised would never do that.

They probably assumed I was a troubled child and a bad influence for their own children, so they abandoned me too...

Rest within the pause of asking yourself, who am I?

— GG

CHAPTER 4
GROUP & GONE

I never fit in there anyways. They were a good hearted Christian family so they didn't kick me out into the streets, they simply took me to a group foster home.

I was about 14 years old and still living in the Richmond Bay Area. The group home was somewhat better than the first foster home experience. There were more kids and a few of them actually liked me.

Still, I never wanted to be there. I was always thinking about my mom and how it could be different living with her.

There were always more rules to be followed and more chores to be done so I was pretty busy in the group home.

Eventually as I warmed up to the new living situation, I made some rebellious friends. I didn't think anyone would ever completely understand me but these kids were different. They could look past my flaws because they just wanted to fit in too.

God is the name of awareness.

Awareness is the eternal presence.

You are that, I Am that.
Now be at peace for there is no one to judge,
because all there is - is yourself. Everywhere.

— GG

It wasn't all sunshine and roses. The majority of kids didn't quite feel me. They would try telling me about time and I would ask them to show me time, because I was always here in the now. It was a confusing concept to me.

During my 14th year, I once again began looking inwardly and started seeing everything as it was without my mind projecting how I wanted things to be. I would ask people if they felt like I felt, I knew there was something greater than us watching over.

Some would listen but the conversation would turn into something else.

I was heavily involved in numerous fights during my stay at the first group home. Being in the area I was growing up in, gang fights and crime were always present. I wasn't an angry teenager, I just wanted to feel accepted and loved.

I couldn't say anything like that where I was from because it would be taken as a sign of weakness but I honestly wanted to belong to something more than myself.

I would stay up at night contemplating how life could be so different if I was understood.

To be nothing
is to be
eternally aware.

— GG

School was never regular for me anymore. Essentially, I dropped out in 2nd grade because I would rather learn from my own experience.

It's inevitable to be influenced and conditioned by ignorance in society, but my witnessing couldn't be contaminated.

I had to go through conditioning and become things I was not in order to survive, though I intuitively knew my soul's perspective would never change.

I started to pray more and more because I had always felt like I was watching the drama of my own movie day in and day out.

Never had I received unconditional support from another individual and that's why I didn't like to depend on anybody. I just yearned to feel wanted in this world.

One day, there was a baseball game that the whole group home went on for a field trip. I didn't feel like going because I had a different plan.

We had the option to either stay home and pass or go to the game – I chose to pass and run away to find my mother.

What is it
that knows and is aware
of experience?

— GG

I remember stealing the group van like it was no big deal. I knew where the keys were and it was too easy for me to snatch them.

I was off to San Francisco to where my mother had been staying. I didn't see her as much anymore but I missed her dearly. I just had this urge to feel my mother again and I sincerely wanted to live with her.

I would follow familiar bus routes and find my way. I mobbed across the golden gate bridge and I was only about 15 at the time.

There was a great sense of freedom to go off on my own and experience the unknown all by myself. I was bumping my favorite E-40 tape and cruising through the city feeling liberated.

My mother wasn't surprised. She told me to go back home. She never understood how much I simply wanted to be in her presence. This time was really tough... Again I felt abandoned.

I had stayed with my mother a couple days until she had to do what she wanted to do without me. So I scurried to the group home and prayed to God I wouldn't be found out. I bustled back as fast and careful as I could in that clunky van.

The way out is within.
Once you are aware of what you really are,
then you realize that all that is,
is within you and you are within all.

And you are all!
And ultimately you see that you alone - exist.

— GG

As I approached familiar grounds and knew I was close, I tried to eject my music. My E-40 tape was jammed and I couldn't get it out of the tape deck! I desperately attempted to pop the tape out but it wouldn't budge!

My return was timed perfectly before I would get in trouble but I had left major evidence in the Van because everyone knew that was my tape.

Of course the counsellors of the group found out. I was sweating profusely when I heard the news. Thankfully no police were called due to my youthful recklessness. I barely knew how to drive.

I was relieved to hear I wasn't in as much trouble as I thought because the counsellor was seeing my mother. I really wanted them to get together so I could see my mom more often but it never really fell through.

When the owner of the home found out what had happened, he wasn't having it.

The counselor was okay with my stunt but it was the owner's final judgment of punishment for me.

The blueprint of life
is awareness of consciousness.
It folds and unfolds
spontaneously and effortlessly.

— GG

CHAPTER 5
ADOLESCENT ASCENSION

Expulsion was the ultimate result of taking the van and they didn't tolerate that. I was introduced to a new group home in the following week.

My next group home was pretty unique. I was 16 years old now and I was involved in a lot more fights.

There was a toxic manager who was a rough military man. He was always bossy and a belligerent old drunk.

I never really found my place here, which I could never find where I truly felt at home.

The other counsellor was a cartoon artist and I admired him for his peaceful work.

I always enjoyed watching him draw and he would teach me a few techniques.

As much as I loved to learn, his practice kept me more centered and present than anything. The art never stuck with me but it helped me cultivate a sense of calm through a creative outlet.

Nothing changes in truth.

As the body-mind,
the seer is experiencing pain and pleasure.

As the non-dual whole-mind, the seer
is experiencing the bliss of being.

As the pure-mind, the seer is experiencing grace
and happiness of being.

As the unaware space,
the seer experiences nothing.

As the aware spacelessness,
the seer is experiencing liberation,
freedom, and spontaneous peace.

— GG

I was involved with a bunch of extracurricular activities at this group home. I remember one time I took a culinary class at the Contra Costa College for baking.

We would always make these wonderful pastries and sweets. Back in the pantries I would find massive bottles of rum that were to be prepared for rum cakes. I couldn't stop drinking dark rum because it was so delicious and I was belligerent drunk.

It turned out that my young body couldn't handle alcohol so I came home drunk for the first time. It was fun while it lasted but I wasn't allowed back in culinary class after swigging on all the rum.

There was a lot of unconscious trauma going down at this group home. One of the owners was the causation of the shutdown. He would put his hands on the children and started choking a kid.

Peace was never found in the facility with the drunk manager either. Eventually, the home came to a closure due to child abuse. And so I was off to my 3rd group home at the age of 17.

In truth,
the one with compassion and wisdom beholds
all beings in the Self
and the Self in all beings;
for that reason - one does not hate anyone.

To the seer,
all things have verily become the Self.
What delusion?
What sorrow can there be
for one who beholds this truth?

— GG

CHAPTER 6
A WHOLE NEW REALITY

The new home was the best! I fit in a lot more and made some friends. It wasn't as strict as the other group homes.

This home was run by 3 younger counsellors no older than their early 30's. There was less parental vision and they didn't force us to go to school.

Instead of giving the kids money for allowance, we received our allowance in marijuana. The counsellors understood our lifestyle and made it convenient because they were selling on the side to keep the group home running.

The downside is that us kids had to hustle harder to get more allowance. Sometimes we would steal from cash registers when the clerk wasn't looking, my friend would use a pin to unlock cash registers and take all the money.

I was in all sorts of trouble around these times. I even started playing with stealing cars. My friends would find a nice car that we could easily open by popping the car lock.

For the seeker after truth,
there is no truth.
Once truth reveals itself from the seeking,
that seeker will vanish.

It is what is untruth that comes and goes.
The truth is never the seeker.

Only truth is eternal.
Truth is AWARENESS of all.
The truth is prior to existence.
To remember who you are
is the ultimate goal.

There is no need for enlightenment
because you are already the light.

— GG

The day I turned 18 was one of the hardest things in a group home. On my birthday was the day one of the counselors asked me if I had anyone picking me up.

I didn't really know where to go anymore because I hadn't seen any family in over 6 years.

I thought I might ask my Auntie Linda if I could stay with her for a few months. I was set on being solo and doing my own thing, but it was some shelter and family to come home to.

My Auntie Linda tried to convert me back into full-on Christian and get me back into religion.

I fell out so much and told her I had my own relationship with God. She never understood my perspective even when I told her that I essentially raised myself and I carry my own experience.

I couldn't be told what to do or how to believe.

I attempted to reach out to my Uncles but they simply cast me away. Family nearby and family in other states were not open to let me in.

There is only YOU -
the indescribable living ecstasy of truth.

You are the SELF -
the eternal witness to all that is known.

You are everywhere
as the core of awareness.

Your light shines like 1000 suns.
You're like the wind
that can never be broken,
like the sky that never changes.

You are the heart of pure bliss.
Untouched by the movements of time,
you are before thought itself.

— GG

CHAPTER 7
THE STREETS OF IGNORANCE

I felt no sense of belonging in this world and I wanted so much to have peace in my life. Anger and loneliness was all I could feel, so I took to the streets.

From learning to steal cars, I would pop locks and use them as my home. And when I couldn't find a home for the night, I would fall asleep on the bus.

Carjacking became a lifestyle. I would take a car for 2-3 days and then be on the hunt for another. My mentality was on pure survival, as long as I had shelter and food I would get by.

This was a harsh reality and it brought me deeper into my sadness, it penetrated into every cell of my body and it propelled my awareness inwards.

I stayed with my cousins quite frequently. They always had clothes and wanted to help me out.

Being swept into their ways of being meant I had to sell drugs. I never really wanted to get into that but I did what I had to.

Balance and love go together.
Love is not a reaction.
If I *love you because you love me,*
that is mere trade -
a thing to be bought in the market;
it is not love.

To love is not to ask anything in return,
not even to feel
that you are giving something.
And it is only such love
that brings balance to light.

— GG

We were called D-Boys. We had this routine down that we felt was fool proof. If we sensed police and didn't want to get caught, we had this system of swallowing our baggie and chasing it down with water to hide the evidence.

I remember I had forgotten my water and had to ditch the rocks because I saw some cops, so I tossed them.

The police witnessed it. They caught me and found my bag. That's when I went to jail for 6 months.

From then on, I was always in and out of jail. That became who I was.

The police got to know me and would address me as Mr. Tate. I would always be found for unauthorized joyriding.

There was a night when I was with some buddies - I could never call anyone my true friend. We were all troubled youths and they decided to rob a lady's purse.

She immediately called the police and they found us before we had thought we got away.

We fought the case for at least 3 weeks but I had too many cases against me. It was time for another 6 months.

*You are the reality
that is manifesting itself.*

— GG

CHAPTER 8
RESTRICTED EXPANSION IN LOVE

Toward the beginning of my confinement experiences, I was placed in a softer Stockton jail called the farm. There was a big white prison bus and a lower level jail we went to in order to clean up.

Community service was always humbling because we were paid 10¢ per hour which I just put on my books for snacks anyways.

My jail buddies were always thinking about girls. Across the jail center was where the female inmates stayed.

All my buddies said a certain girl liked me and we silently admired each other from afar. I was still too shy to approach and rather discouraged from all my trials and tribulations.

We couldn't really talk but I decided to write her a note. We began a sacred exchange of letters and soon we were always writing to each other.

Her name was Jess and she was beautiful. In my world of struggle, I felt that I could finally open up my heart of authenticity to express my true self in her light.

The nature of the body is mind.
The nature of the mind is consciousness.
The nature of consciousness is awareness.
The nature of awareness is pure knowing
in which all experience is known.

— GG

From across the yard, we would ghost hug because we were segregated by fences. We couldn't really have any public affection but we would always flirt a little, knowing we couldn't ever touch.

One day, we were talking and we saw an open bathroom. The guards must've been off duty. Jess and I decided to break for the stall and sneak a quick kiss before anyone could see! We had no time to talk about it, but our silent admiration said everything.

My silent aloneness began to break. I could feel my lonely awareness bloom into a love that knew no boundaries.

Jess would tell me to do push-ups and I would try to impress her as best I could. I was only 19 and she was 18 at the time. We were just kids falling in love.

The hate and disgust I had experienced in jail had gracefully dissolved because I found new life in the recognition of my own sweetness.

Sometimes we would get in trouble and we would sweep the yard at night. I would sweep towards her unit and that was the time for us to have conversations.

I, *is consciousness.*
I AM, *is the conscious experience.*
I *need this and* I *desire that,*
is consciousness dreaming.
I AM *nothing,*
is consciousness awakening to itself.

— GG

A great change had occurred within my being because I realized this love was only a reflection of my potential.

Now my true heart was made manifest and was shown to me as the seed of love that I am. I began to grow as a human faster than ever because I was in love.

You are the eternal being.
There is no need
to prove or believe in anything.

You are the flawless diamond,
infinite light that shines timelessly.

Love is who you are,
for there is only you that exists
everywhere as Shiva.

— GG

CHAPTER 9
FINAL CYCLES

Every time I went back to jail seemed like a continuing never-ending nightmare.

All I remember was crying and being in deep prayer. I never liked being in jail and I started to have a disheartening emotional breakdown.

I had shivering sweats and I couldn't stop my mind from battling the acceptance of where I was. My actions had led me to this moment of deep seated regret.

Being in jail was like being in hate central. There was so much disgust projected from each individual and their click, so much division and control.

I always had to keep my guard up and put my tough guy face on. I hated pretending to be a man of hate just to survive.

My last term in jail was 3 years and the worst. I was forced to take antidepressant drugs and I started to go blind. I couldn't stop thinking about why and how I had returned.

No one has problems.
Problems are created by your own thoughts
and the illusion of time,
past and future.

— GG

I was releasing my conditioned way of thinking and disem-
powered habits before being arrested for taking a bottle of
Tylenol because I was sick and had no money to pay for it
and just needed to feel better so I could work.

You are the only consciousness,
not this or that.
Everything that appears,
appears within you.
Everything that arises,
arises within you.

You are here, you have no purpose.
You are fearless, timeless, know minded,
pure loving awareness.

— GG

CHAPTER 10
THE COMMITMENT TO THE PATH

After my final jail visit was over, I had a twelve step program to attend. I really didn't align with it but I eventually went through with most of it. I knew in my being that I was finished with being the old conditioned self I had been for so long.

I was now 33 years old.

Jess had become an administrator of sober living homes for 7 different homes. She helped me get a home and we started to connect with more authenticity than ever before.

We used to go to Laguna Beach at the Chakra Shack. We would go into the float tanks to experiment with sense deprivation. I was really drawn to the profound peace that being in total silence and darkness provided me.

The remembrance of my nature as a calm presence had always stuck with me but now I wanted to go deeper and I was ready for it. I would always visit the float tanks to feel a contentment of feeling home in my soul.

To *find your true Self*,
*you must first stop listening
to the mind so much*...
*and start listening
to the silence of your heart*.

— GG

The place also had a vegan burger cafe. One time while eating out, we came to the realization that this was the type of lifestyle we wanted to live. The vibes from the areas we visited made us feel overwhelmingly happy and fulfilled.

From that realization, I decided to start getting into the marijuana business. I wanted to share this peace I had revived within my being and start creating the abundance I knew I was worthy of.

We ended up speaking to investors and founded Sticky Leaves. The investors really look notice of the uprising of the marijuana business.

One investor in particular really wanted to get into the business and we said we were experienced. We made it happen and sure enough we were creating the dream reality we believed we could have.

As we started to cultivate more of the feeling of abundance and let go of scarcity, the path of deepening our connection to spirit was illuminated for us.

Once the mind has become still,
conditioning will slowly
start to lose its power
and gradually return to its natural state
of peace, openness, transparency,
availability, sensitivity, and love.

— GG

Jess and I committed to the spiritual path together and wanted to share as much love as we could so everyone we encountered would feel free and peaceful. We decided to fully integrate our spiritual nature and live the most high vibrational life we could imagine.

It was now 2010. I remember catching my first video of Mooji Baba and it really captivated my heart. For once, I felt understood as if someone could relate to the same experience I had been having my whole life.

Osho was another teacher I found very valuable. He was known as the rich man's guru but I understood what he was conveying. He was the living truth of the same thing I was experiencing since I was 5 years old.

I wasn't interested in the spiritual path or any teachings. It was an experiential feeling rather than concepts to grasp.

If I heard someone speaking of awareness, I would feel so relatable because I would know by my own experience.

Consciousness does not love,
it is love itself.
It is existence itself.
It does not know, it is knowledge itself.

— GG

CHAPTER 11
HERE I AM

Being aware of being aware is the feeling of being detached from the body.

Truth is everywhere and within everyone.

I have fully embraced the purpose of being a divine instrument for love to flow through me in any form of natural compassionate expression.

There is no teaching I have to share, no words can suffice the transcendental realization that each human is capable of attaining.

I can only share what is true to me and my own experience is the ultimate authority. There is no dogma to push, no concept to conceive... Only an awareness to innerstand.

Every religion for me has been some form of explanation or path to realize heaven within but it is not necessary to have a set path.

Only when you relax, you begin to vibrate with the reality of truth.

There is no universe without consciousness.
Consciousness is the universe.
The universe is consciousness. Consciousness is the real I AM.

— GG

That's why I share unteaching, that's why I celebrate in un-conditioning. As we let go of old identities, old stories, fears, traumas and doubts that hold us back from happiness – we start to perceive the truth that we are not separate from each other.

I have hosted many retreats to share the healing medicine of living meditation. I love to be of service, to be a vessel of un-chained and unconditioned divine love – because that's what everyone truly is.

My friends call me good guru, but I know I have no name. I know that only when I do not know, I can be open to the unknown. When I trust in the uncertainty, I am met with the extraordinary miracles and challenges that the almighty unity has for me.

As the witness of the thought process without the identity of the doer, I know I am a human who is just being – just like you. And when we come back to the basics of just being… we return to our preeminent nature of eternal loving awareness.

My name is Alonzo Tate. This is my story of awakening and realizing the one consciousness that fills every heartbeat with wholeness.

I AM, *presence.*
I AM, *loving awareness.*

— GG

CONNECT WITH THE AUTHOR

Alonzo Tate "Good Guru," is a heart-centered being who shares the truth of his experience. He is a compassionate soul that loves helping others realize their potential.

He is on the path to create healing centers around the Washington State area to assist humanity in coming home to themselves.

His vision is to create more peace in the world through the art of meditation, celebration, and self-inquiry.

You can follow his journey and his service on Facebook.

Go to:
https://www.facebook.com/
The-Good-Guru-115948969848431/

Made in the USA
Columbia, SC
19 December 2020

28762977R00046